Ed Franklin

Wood Pellet Smoker and Grill

Cookbook

**Delicious Recipes
for Flavorful Barbecue**

Contents

Smoking Tips and Tricks

Selecting a Smoker

Electric Smokers

The electric smoker is the best smoker because it is very simple to use. Just set it, put your food in it and leave the rest of the work to the smoker. There is nothing an electric smoker cannot grill, be it seafood, poultry, meat, cheese, or bread. It requires little attention unlike other smokers like filling water bin, lighting Preferred Wood Pellet or charcoal and checking on fuel frequently. Yes, unlike traditional smoker, electric smoker just needs 2 to 4 ounce of Preferred Wood Pellet chips that turns out a delicious and flavorful smoky food. Furthermore, they maintain cooking Smoke Temperature well. On the other hand, it sleek and stylish look and small size make it appropriate if you are living in an apartment or condo. Due to their simpler functions and hassle-free cooking, the electric smoker is a good choice for beginner cooks who want to get started with smoking food.

Gas Smokers

Gas smokers or propane smoker are much like a gas grill using propane as a fuel. Therefore, Preferred Wood Pellet for cooking remains consistent and steady. Furthermore, gas smokers are as easy to use, just set the Smoke Temperature and walk away. However, frequent checks need to be done to make sure fuel does not run out. It is not a big issue, but one should keep in mind. And the best part, a gas smoker can be used when there is no electricity or when you need an oven. A gas smoker can take up to cooking Smoke Temperature to 450 degrees, making this smoker flexible to be used as an oven. Another fantastic feature of gas smoker is its portability so they can use anywhere. Just pack it and take it along with you on your camping trips or other outdoor adventures.

Charcoal Smokers

Nothing can beat the flavor charcoal gives to your food. Its best flavor just simply cannot match with any other smoker flavor. Unfortunately, setting a charcoal smoker, tuning fuel, maintaining cooking Smoke Temperature, and checking food can be a pain and you might burn the food. Not to worry, these hassles of a charcoal smoker does go away with practice and experience. Therefore, a charcoal smoker suits perfectly for serious grillers and barbecue purist who want flavors.

Pellet Smokers

Pellet smokers are making a surge due to their best feature of a pallet of maintaining a consistent Smoke Temperature. It contains an automated system to drop pallets which frees the cook to monitor fuel level. The addition of thermostat gives the user the complete control the cooking Smoke Temperature and grilling of food under ideal condition. In addition, the smoking food uses Preferred Wood Pellet from Preferred Wood Pellet which gives food a delicious flavor. The only downside of pallet smoker is their high cost between the ranges of $100 to %600.

Choose the Right Preferred Wood Pellet

Smoker Preferred Wood Pellet is an important element which you need to decide correctly to cook a delicious smoked food. The reason is that smoker chips of Preferred Wood Pellets impart different flavors on the food you are cooking in the smoker. Therefore, you should know which smoker Preferred Wood Pellet should be used to create a delicious smoked food. Here is the lowdown of smoker Preferred Wood Pellets and which food is best with them.

1- Alder: A lighter smoker Preferred Wood Pellet with natural sweetness.

Best to smoke: Any fish especially salmon, poultry, and game birds.

2- Maple: This smoker Preferred Wood Pellet has a mild and sweet flavor. In addition, its sweet smoke gives the food a dark appearance. For better flavor, use it as a combination with alder, apple, or oak smoker Preferred Wood Pellets.

Best to smoke: Vegetables, cheese, and poultry.

3- Apple: A mild fruity flavor smoker Preferred Wood Pellet with natural sweetness. When mixed with oak smoker Preferred Wood Pellet, it gives a great flavor to food. Let food smoke for several hours as the smoke takes a while to permeate the food with the flavors.

Best to smoke: Poultry, beef, pork, lamb, and seafood.

4- Cherry: This smoker Preferred Wood Pellet is an all-purpose fruity flavor Preferred Wood Pellet for any type of meat. Its smoke gives the food a rich, mahogany color. Try smoking by mixing it with alder, oak, pecan, and hickory smoker Preferred Wood Pellet.

Best to smoke: Chicken, turkey, ham, pork, and beef.

5- Oak: Oak Preferred Wood Pellet gives a medium flavor to food which is stronger compared to apple Preferred Wood Pellet and cherry Preferred Wood Pellet and lighter compared to hickory. This versatile smoker Preferred Wood Pellet works well blended with hickory, apple, and cherry Preferred Wood Pellets.

Best to smoke: Sausages, brisket, and lamb.

6- Peach and Pear: Both smoker Preferred Wood Pellets are like each other. They give food a subtle light and fruity flavor with the addition of natural sweetness.

Best to smoke: Poultry, pork, and game birds.

7- Hickory: Hickory Preferred Wood Pellet infuses a strong sweet and bacon flavor into the food, especially meat cuts. Do not over smoke with this Preferred Wood Pellet as it can turn the taste of food bitter.

Best to smoke: Red meat, poultry, pork shoulder, ribs.

8- Pecan: This sweet smoker Preferred Wood Pellet lends the food a rich and nutty flavor. Use it with Mesquite Preferred Wood Pellet to balance its sweetness.

Best to smoke: Poultry, pork.

9- Walnut: This strong flavored smoker Preferred Wood Pellet is often used as a mixing Preferred Wood Pellet due to its slightly bitter flavor. Use walnut Preferred Wood Pellet with lighter smoke Preferred Wood Pellets like pecan Preferred Wood Pellet or apple Preferred Wood Pellet.

Best to smoke: Red meat and game birds.

10-   Grape: Grape Preferred Wood Pellet chips give a sweet berry flavor to food. It is best to use these Preferred Wood Pellet chips with apple Preferred Wood Pellet chips.

Best to smoke: Poultry

11-   Mulberry: Mulberry Preferred Wood Pellet chips is like apple Preferred Wood Pellet chips. It adds natural sweetness and gives berry finish to the food.

Best to smoke: Ham and Chicken.

12-   Mesquite: Mesquite Preferred Wood Pellet chips flavor is earthy and slightly harsh and bitter. It burns fast and strongly hot. Therefore, do not use it for longer grilling.

Best to smoke: Red meat, dark meat.

Select the Meat

Choose the type of meat which tastes good with a smoky flavor. Following meat goes well for smoking.

Beef: ribs, brisket, and corned beef.

Pork: spareribs, roast, shoulder, and ham.

Poultry: whole chicken, whole turkey, and big game hens.

Seafood: Salmon, scallops, trout, and lobster.

Getting Meat Ready

Prepare meat according to the recipe. Sometimes meat is cured, marinated, or simply seasoned with the rub. These preparation directions ensure smoked meat turn out flavorful, tender, and extremely juicy.

Brine is a solution to treating poultry, pork, or ham. It involves dissolving brine ingredients in water poured into a huge container and then adding meat to it. Then let soak for at least 8 hours and after that, rinse it well and pat dry before you begin smoking.

Marinate treat beef or briskets and add flavors to it. It is better to make deep cuts in meat to let marinate ingredients deep into it. Drain meat or smoke it straightaway.

Rubs are commonly used to treat beef, poultry, or ribs. They are a combination of salt and many spices, rubbed generously all over the meat. Then the meat is left to rest for at least 2 hours or more before smoking it.

Before smoking meat, make sure it is at room Smoke Temperature. This ensures meat is cooked evenly and reach its internal Smoke Temperature at the end of smoking time.

Placing Meat into the Smoker

Do not place the meat directly overheat into the smoker because the main purpose of smoking is cooking meat at low Smoke Temperature. Set aside your fuel on one side of the smoker and place meat on the other side and let cook.

Smoking time: The smoking time of meat depends on the internal Smoke Temperature. For this, use a meat thermometer and insert it into the thickest part of the meat. The smoking time also varies with the size of meat. Check recipes to determine the exact smoking time for the meat.

Pork

1. Smoked Pork Tenderloins

Preparation Time: 20 minutes

Cooking Time: 1½ hours

Servings: 4 to 6 for each pork tenderloin

Smoke Temperature: 225°F, 375°F

Preferred Wood Pellet: Hickory, Apple

Ingredients:

2 (1½ to 2-pound) pork tenderloins

Cup roasted garlic–seasoned extra-virgin olive oil

Cup Jan's Original Dry Rub or Pork Dry Rub

Directions:

Preparing for the Grill

Trim any overabundance fat and silver skin from the meat.

Rub sides of the tenderloins with the olive oil and residue with the rub.

Wrap the seasoned tenderloins in plastic coating and refrigerate for 2 to 4 hours.

Structure the Smoker grill for a non-direct cooking and preheat to 230°F using hickory or apple pellets.

Remove the plastic coating from the meat and supplement your Smoker grill probes or a remote meat probe into the thickest bit of each tenderloin. In case your grill does not have meat probe capacities, or you do not guarantee a remote meat probe by then use a minute read automated thermometer during the cook for internal Smoke Temperature readings.

Place the tenderloins on the grill and smoke them for 45 minutes at 230°F.

Increase the pit Smoke Temperature to 360°F and wrap up the tenderloins for around 45 other zone reaches 145°F.

Rest the pork tenderloins under a free foil tent for 10 minutes before serving.

2. Pulled Hickory-Smoked Pork Butts

Preparation Time: 30 to 45 minutes

Cooking Time: 6 hours

Servings: at least 20

Smoke Temperature: 225°F, 375°F

Preferred Wood Pellet: Hickory

Ingredients:

2 (10-pound) boneless pork butts, vacuum-stuffed or fresh

1 cup roasted garlic–seasoned extra-virgin olive oil

¾ cup Pork Dry Rub, Jan's Original Dry Rub, or your preferred pork rub

Directions:

Trim the fat cap and any effectively available enormous segments of abundance fat from every pork butt as you see fit. Some pit masters prefer to reduce the fat cap to ¼ inch or leave the whole fat cap on because they accept that the liquefying fat seasons the butts as they cook. This technique restrains the development of bark in regions secured by fat. In this way I prescribe evacuating the fat cap to boost the measure of treasured bark.

Cut every pork butt down the middle. Use silicone nourishment grade cooking groups or butcher's twine to hold the meat together during cooking and taking care of.

Rub every one of the sides of every pork butt with the oil. Sprinkle every pork butt with a liberal measure of the rub and pat it in with your hand.

Independently double wrap the seasoned boneless pork butts firmly in plastic wrap and refrigerate medium-term.

Design the Smoker grill for a non-direct cooking and preheat to 225°F utilizing hickory pellets.

Supplement your Smoker grill meat probes or a remote meat probe into the thickest piece of at least one pork butts.

Smoke the pork butts for 3 hours.

Take care to ensure that you keep your meat probes in the butts as you double-wrap them.

Keep cooking the foil-wrapped pork butts until the internal Smoke Temperature of the pork butts arrives at 200°F to 205°F.

Remove the pork butts and FTC them for 3 to 4 hours before pulling and serving.

Force the smoked pork butts into minimal succulent shreds utilizing your preferred pulling technique. I prefer utilizing my hands while wearing heat-safe gloves.

On the off chance that you would like, blend the pulled pork butts with any remaining fluids.

Serve the pulled pork with grill sauce on a fresh-prepared move topped with coleslaw.

3. Pork Sirloin Tip Roast Three Ways

Preparation Time: 20 minutes

Cooking Time: 1½ to 3 hours

Servings: 4 to 6

Smoke Temperature: 225°F, 375°F

Preferred Wood Pellet: Hickory

Ingredients:

¾ cup 100% apple juice

2 tablespoons roasted garlic–seasoned extra-virgin olive oil

5 tablespoons Pork Dry Rub or a business rubs, for example, Plowboys BBQ Bovine Bold

Directions:

Dry the roast with a piece of paper

Utilize a flavor/marinade injector to infuse all zones of tip roast with the apple juice.

Rub the whole roast with the olive oil and afterward cover generously with the rub.

Utilize 2 silicone nourishment grade cooking groups or butcher's twine to support the roast.

Design the Smoker grill for a non-direct cooking and preheat to 350°F utilizing apple pellets.

Remove the plastic wrap and supplement your Smoker grill meat probe or a remote meat probe into the thickest piece of the roast. If your grill does not have meat probe capabilities, or you do not claim a remote meat probe, at that point utilize a moment read computerized thermometer during the cook for internal Smoke Temperature readings.

Roast the meat until the internal Smoke Temperature arrives at 145°F, about 1½ hours.

Rest the roast under a free foil tent for 15 minutes.

Remove the cooking groups or twine and cut the roast contrary to what would be expected.

4. Smoked Pork Sausage

Preparation time: 29 hours

Cooking time: 3 hours.

Servings: 6

Smoke Temperature: 225°F, 375°F

Preferred Wood Pellet: Hickory

Ingredients:

2 pounds pork butt, cubed

1/2-pound pork fat, cubed

1/2 teaspoon onion powder

1/2 teaspoon garlic powder

1 tablespoon sea salt

1 1/2 teaspoons ground black pepper

1 teaspoon brown sugar

1/4 teaspoon cayenne pepper

1 1/2 teaspoons dried oregano

1/4 cup water

Directions:

Take hog casings, place them in a large bowl, pour in water, and let soak for 1 hour.

Meanwhile, place pork butt and fat in a food processor, process until grind and place in a large bowl.

Season with onion powder, garlic powder, salt, black pepper, sugar, cayenne pepper and oregano, and mix until well combined, set aside in refrigerator until required.

Rinse hog casings, then working on one casing at a time, tie one end of the casing and another open end over the nozzle and slowly push meat mixture into the casing until filled.

Do not overstuff the casing and once it is filled, tie the other end as well and then tie sausage roll every 4 inches by twisting the basing.

Air dries the casing for 1 to 3 hours or rotate casing on paper towel often to dry its surfaces.

Then take an enormous container, layer its bottom with some paper towels, then top with sausage, add more paper towels and then more sausage until container is full.

Cover container with lid and place in the refrigerator for 12 to 24 hours or until chilled.

When ready to cook, place chilled sausage for 20 to 30 minutes or until their Smoke Temperature reach room Smoke Temperature.

Meanwhile, plug in the smoker, fill its tray with hickory Preferred Wood Pellet chips and water pan halfway through, and place dripping pan above the water pan.

Then open the top vent, shut with lid, and use Smoke Temperature settings to preheat smoker at 250 degrees F.

In the meantime, cut sausage at the twisted sections and remove their ties.

Place sausage on smoker rack, insert a meat thermometer, then shut with lid and set the timer to smoke for 3 hours or more until meat thermometer registers an internal Smoke Temperature of 165 degrees F.

Check vent of smoker every hour and add more Preferred Wood Pellet chips and water to maintain Smoke Temperature and smoke.

Serve straightaway.

Preparation time: 12 hours and 20 minutes.

Cooking time: 8 hours.

Servings: 16

Smoke Temperature: 225°F, 375°F

Preferred Wood Pellet: Hickory

Ingredients:

8-pound pork butt roast, fat trimmed

2 tablespoons onion powder

2 tablespoons garlic powder

1/4 cup sea salt

1/2 cup brown sugar

1 tablespoon ground black pepper

1 tablespoon paprika

1 tablespoon dried thyme

1 tablespoon dried oregano

6 tablespoons yellow mustard BBQ sauce for serving

Burger rolls for serving

Directions:

Rinse pork, pat dry and then rub with mustard.

Stir together remaining ingredients and sprinkle the spice mixture all over the pork until evenly coated.

Transfer pork roast into a foil pan, fat-side up, cover with plastic wrap and let marinate in the refrigerator for 8 to 12 hours.

Then remove pork from the pan and let rest at room Smoke Temperature for 30 minutes.

In the meantime, plug in the smoker, fill its tray with hickory Preferred Wood Pellet chips and water pan halfway through, and place dripping pan above the water pan.

Then open the top vent, shut with lid, and use Smoke Temperature settings to preheat smoker at 225 degrees F.

Place pork on smoker rack, insert a meat thermometer, then shut with lid and set the timer to smoke for 8 hours or more until meat thermometer registers an internal Smoke Temperature of 190 degrees F.

Check vent of smoker every hour and add more Preferred Wood Pellet chips and water to maintain Smoke Temperature and smoke.

When done, transfer pork to a cutting board, let rest for 20 minutes and then shred with two forks.

Evenly divide shredded pork on buns, top with BBQ sauce and serve.

6. Smoked Bologna

Preparation time: 30 minutes.

Cooking time: 4 hours.

Servings: 12

Smoke Temperature: 225°F, 375°F

Preferred Wood Pellet: Hickory

Ingredients:

3 pounds bologna roll

2 tablespoons ground black pepper

3/4 cup brown sugar

1/4 cup yellow mustard

Directions:

Plug in the smoker, fill its tray with apple Preferred Wood Pellet chips and water pan halfway through, and place dripping pan above the water pan.

Then open the top vent, shut with lid, and use Smoke Temperature settings to preheat smoker at 225 degrees F.

In the meantime, score bologna with ¼ inch deep diamond pattern, then coats with mustard and season with black pepper and sugar.

Place bologna on smoker rack, insert a meat thermometer, then shut with lid and set the timer to smoke for 3 to 4 hours.

Check vent of smoker every hour and add more Preferred Wood Pellet chips and water to maintain Smoke Temperature and smoke.

When done, transfer bologna to a cutting board, let cool for 15 minutes and then cut into ½ inch thick slices.

Serve bologna slices as sandwiches.

7.   Smoked Pork Shoulder

Preparation time: 9 hours and 15 minutes.

Cooking time: 8 hours.

Servings: 12

Smoke Temperature: 225°F, 375°F

Preferred Wood Pellet: Hickory

Ingredients:

8-pound pork shoulder roast, bone-in, and fat trimmed

2 teaspoons onion powder

2 teaspoons garlic powder

2 teaspoons celery salt

4 teaspoons salt

2 teaspoons ground black pepper

1/4 cup brown sugar

1/2 teaspoon cayenne pepper

1/2 cup paprika

2 teaspoons dry mustard

Directions:

Rinse pork shoulder, pat dry thoroughly with paper towels and place roast in a foil pan.

Stir together remaining ingredients until mixed and then season roast with the spice mixture until evenly coated.

Cover pan tightly with plastic wrap and let marinate in the refrigerator for 8 hours.

Then remove pork from refrigerator and let rest for 1 hour at room Smoke Temperature.

Meanwhile, plug in the smoker, fill its tray with hickory Preferred Wood Pellet chips and water pan halfway through, and place dripping pan above the water pan.

Then open the top vent, shut with lid, and use Smoke Temperature settings to preheat smoker at 225 degrees F.

Place pork on smoker rack, insert a meat thermometer, then shut with lid and set the timer to smoke for 8 hours or more until meat thermometer registers an internal Smoke Temperature of 190 degrees F.

Check vent of smoker every hour and add more Preferred Wood Pellet chips and water to maintain Smoke Temperature and smoke.

When done, transfer pork to a cutting board, cover with aluminum foil and let rest for 30 minutes.

Then remove bone from the pork, slice thinly and serve.

8.   Spiced Pork Loin

Preparation time: 1 hour and 45 minutes.

Cooking time: 3 hours.

Servings: 12

Smoke Temperature: 225°F, 375°F

Preferred Wood Pellet: Hickory

Ingredients:

6-pound pork loin, boneless

1/2 teaspoon garlic powder

2 teaspoons sea salt

1 teaspoon ground black pepper

1 tablespoon Chinese five spice powder

2 tablespoons olive oil

Directions:

Rinse pork, pat dry with paper towels and place on a foil pan.

Stir together remaining ingredients until smooth paste form, then rub this paste on all sides of pork and let marinate for 60 minutes at room Smoke Temperature.

Meanwhile, plug in the smoker, fill its tray with oak Preferred Wood Pellet chips and water pan halfway through, and place dripping pan above the water pan.

Then open the top vent, shut with lid, and use Smoke Temperature settings to preheat smoker at 225 degrees F.

Place pork on smoker rack, insert a meat thermometer, then shut with lid and set the timer to smoke for 3 hours or more until meat thermometer registers an internal Smoke Temperature of 155 degrees F.

Check vent of smoker every hour and add more Preferred Wood Pellet chips and water to maintain Smoke Temperature and smoke.

When done, transfer pork to a cutting board, cover with aluminum foil, and let rest for 30 minutes.

When done, transfer pork to a cutting board, cover with aluminum foil, and let rest for 30 minutes.

Slice pork into ½ inch thick pieces and serve.

9. Stuffed Porchetta

Preparation time: 10 minutes.

Cooking time: 20 minutes.

Servings: 12

Smoke Temperature: 225°F, 375°F

Preferred Wood Pellet: Hickory

Ingredients:

6 pounds pork belly, fat trimmed

12-ounce sundried tomato spread

2 cups giardiniera, Chicago styled

1 cup bacon jam

½ cup dry rub

Directions:

Plug in the smoker, fill its tray with oak Preferred Wood Pellet chips and water pan halfway through, and place dripping pan above the water pan.

Then open the top vent, shut with lid, and use Smoke Temperature settings to preheat smoker at 275 degrees F.

In the meantime, rinse pork, pat dry and then season with dry rub on all sides until evenly coated.

Place seasoned pork on a cutting board or clean working space; spread tomato spread on top, layer with giardiniera and tomato spread, then roll pork and tie with kitchen twines.

Place stuffed pork on smoker rack, insert a meat thermometer, then shut with lid and set the timer to smoke for 2 to 3 hours or more until meat thermometer registers an internal Smoke Temperature of 195 degrees F.

Check vent of smoker every hour and add more Preferred Wood Pellet chips and water to maintain Smoke Temperature and smoke.

When done, transfer porchetta to a cutting board, let rest for 15 minutes and then slice to serve.

Beef

10. BBQ Chili Burger

Preparation Time: 20 minutes

Cooking Time: 1 hour and 30 minutes

Servings: 4-6 people

Smoke Temperature: 180°F and 375°F

Preferred Wood Pellet: Hickory

Ingredients:

Beef Chili

2.5 Lbs. Ground Beef

1 Large Onion, Diced

1 Tsp Kosher Salt

1 Can Chipotles in Adobo, Minced with Sauce

1/4 Cup Chili Powder

1-1/2 Tbsp Cumin Powder

3 Cloves Garlic, Peeled and Minced

1 Jalapeño Pepper, Minced

1 (14 Oz) Can Diced or Crushed Tomatoes

2 Cups Chicken Stock

1/8 Cup Flour

1/2 Tbsp Dark Chili Powder

1/2 Tbsp Ground Cinnamon

Juice of 1 Lime

1 Hershey's Chocolate Bar

Salt and Pepper, To Taste

Chili Burgers

2 Lbs. Ground Beef

Traeger Beef Rub, As Needed

2 Cups Beef Chili or Preferred Chili

5 Hamburger Buns

5 Slices Cheddar Cheese

1 Red Onion, Sliced

1 Bag Frito Corn Chips

Directions:

For the Beef Chili: Heat a large Dutch oven on the stove top over medium-high heat. Cook the ground beef until browned and cooked through.

Add all chili Ingredients: minus the chocolate and limes to the Dutch oven.

When ready to cook, start the Traeger according to grill Direction. Set the Smoke Temperature to 350 degrees F and preheat, lid closed for 10 to 15 minutes.

Put the Dutch oven into the grill for 2 hours, stirring every hour. Remove Dutch oven from grill.

Stir the lime juice and the chocolate into the chili. Set chili aside until ready to assemble the burgers.

For the burgers: When ready to cook, set the Smoke Temperature to 350°F and preheat, lid closed for 15 minutes.

Form into 5 equal patties and season both sides with Traeger Beef Rub.

Place patties directly on the grill grate and cook for 4-5 minutes per side, flipping once. Top each burger with cheese and cook for 1 minute more to melt.

Remove from the grill and let rest 1-2 minutes.

To build burger, place the patty on the bottom bun, add a scoop of chili, Fritos, red onion, and finish with the top bun. Enjoy

11. Perfectly Grilled Steaks

Preparation Time: an hour

Cooking Time: 15 minutes

Servings: 2

Smoke Temperature: 180°F and 375°F

Preferred Wood Pellet: Any

Ingredients:

2 USDA Choice or Prime 1¼ to 1½-inch-thick New York strip steaks (around 12 to 14 ounces every) extra-virgin olive oil

4 teaspoons Pete's Western Rub or salt and pepper, partitioned

Directions:

Remove the steaks from the refrigerator and spread freely with plastic wrap around 45 minutes before cooking to carry them to room Smoke Temperature.

When the steaks arrive at room Smoke Temperature, brush them on the two sides with olive oil.

Flavor each side of the steaks with 1 teaspoon of rubbing or salt and pepper, and afterward let remain at room Smoke Temperature for in any event 5 minutes before grilling.

Arrange the Smoker grill for direct cooking by utilizing burning grates, set the Smoke Temperature to high, and preheat to at any rate 450°F using any pellets.

Place the meat on the grill and cook on one side until marginally seared, 2 to 3 minutes.

On a similar side, rotate the steaks 90 degrees for cross grill stamps, and cook for an extra 2 to 3 minutes.

Flip the meat over and grill until they arrive at desired doneness:

3 to 5 minutes for medium uncommon (an internal Smoke Temperature of 135°F)

6 to 8 minutes for medium (an internal Smoke Temperature of 140°F)

8 to 11 minutes for medium-well (an internal Smoke Temperature of 150°F)

Move the steaks to a platter, tent freely with foil, and let rest 5 minutes before serving.

12. Smoked Tri-Tip Roast

Preparation Time: 20 minutes (in addition to medium-term marinating)

Cooking Time: 2 hours

Rest Time: 15 minutes

Servings: 4-6

Smoke Temperature: 180°F and 375°F

Preferred Wood Pellet: Hickory, Blend

Ingredients:

1 (2½ to 3-pound) entire peeled tri-tip roast

3 tablespoons roasted garlic–enhanced extra-virgin olive oil

3 tablespoons Pete's Western Rub or your preferred Santa Maria–style rub

Directions:

Rub sides of the tri-tip with the olive oil and afterward with the Pete's Western Rub or other rub.

Twofold wrap the seasoned tri-tip roast with plastic wrap and refrigerate medium-term.

Design the Smoker grill for indirect heat and preheat to 180°F utilizing hickory pellets or a mix.

On the off chance that your unit has one, embed your Smoker grill meat test into the thickest piece of the tri-tip roast and smoke for 60 minutes.

After 60 minutes, increase the pit Smoke Temperature to 325°F. Cook until the internal Smoke Temperature arrives at 140° to 145°F.

Rest the smoked tri-tip under a free foil tent for 15 minutes before serving.

Cut the roast contrary to what would be expected utilizing the representation underneath as a guide.

13. Meaty Chuck Short Ribs

Preparation Time: 20 minutes

Cooking Time: 5 to 6 hours

Servings: 2-4

Smoke Temperature: 180°F and 375°F

Preferred Wood Pellet: Mesquite, Hickory

Ingredients:

English-cut 4-bone chunk meat throws short ribs

3 to 4 tablespoons extra-virgin olive or yellow mustard

3 to 5 tablespoons Pete's Western Rub

Directions:

Trim the fat top from the ribs, leaving a ¼ inch fat, and remove any silver skin.

Remove the membrane from the bones to season the meat appropriately by working a spoon handle under the membrane to get a piece lifted. Utilize a paper towel to snatch the membrane and force it off the bones.

Slather olive oil or the mustard on all sides of the short rib section, season generously on all sides with the rub.

Design the Smoker grill for indirect heat and preheat to 225°F utilizing mesquite or hickory pellets.

Supplement your Smoker grill or a remote meat probe into the thickest piece of the section of ribs. If your grill does not have meat probe abilities, or you do not claim a remote meat probe, at that point utilize a moment read computerized thermometer during the cook for internal Smoke Temperature readings.

Place the ribs bone-side down on the grill and smoke at 225°F for 5 hours.

If after 5 hours the ribs have not arrived at an internal Smoke Temperature of in any event 195°F, at that point increase the pit Smoke Temperature to 250°F until the internal Smoke Temperature arrives at 195° to 205°F.

Rest the smoked short ribs under a free foil tent for 15 minutes before serving...

14. Texas-Style Brisket Flat

Preparation Time: 45 minutes

Cooking Time: 5 to 6 hours

Servings: 8-10

Smoke Temperature: 180°F and 375°F

Preferred Wood Pellet: Mesquite, Oak

Ingredients:

6½ pound beef brisket level

Cup roasted garlic–enhanced extra-virgin olive oil

Cup Texas-Style Brisket Rub or your preferred brisket rub

Directions:

Trim the fat top off the brisket and remove any silver skin.

Rub the trimmed meat on sides with the olive oil.

Apply the rub to sides of the brisket, guaranteeing that it is wholly verified with the rub.

Double-wrap the brisket in plastic coating and refrigerate medium-term for the rub to enter the meat or, if you like, you can cook the brisket immediately.

Remove the brisket from the refrigerator and expand your Smoker grill or a remote meat probe into the thickest bit of the meat. If your grill does not have meat probe, capacities or you do not have a remote meat probe, by then use a minute read propelled thermometer during the cook for internal Smoke Temperature readings.

Arrange the Smoker grill for a non-direct cooking and preheat to 250°F using mesquite or oak pellets.

Smoke the brisket at 260°F, until the internal Smoke Temperature lands at 160°F (around 4 hours).

Remove the brisket from the grill, double-wrap it in heavy-duty aluminum foil, attempting to keep the meat probe in place, and put it back in the smoker-grill.

Increase the pit Smoke Temperature to 330°F and cook the brisket until the internal Smoke Temperature lands at 205°F, about an extra 2 hours.

Remove the foiled brisket, bandage it in a towel, and place it in cooler, implying the FTC guidelines on. Let sit in the cooler for 3 to 4 hours earlier cutting in opposition to what might be reasonable and serving.

Poultry

15. Turmeric Chicken

Preparation time: 10 minutes

Cooking Time: 35 minutes

Servings: 4

Smoke Temperature: 180°F and 375°F

Preferred Wood Pellet: Mesquite, Oak

Ingredients:

Salt

One t. turmeric

½ c. bacon fat

4 cloves minced garlic

4 chicken breasts

Directions:

Put the chicken breasts into a large shallow dish.

In another bowl, put the garlic, turmeric, bacon fat, and salt. Stir well to combine.

Rub each chicken breast generously with the mixture.

Add Preferred Wood Pellet pellets to your smoker and follow your cooker's startup procedure. Preheat your smoker, with your lid closed, until it reaches 350.

For about 10 mins. smoke the chicken on the grill. Flip them and smoke for ten minutes more.

16. Mediterranean Chicken

Preparation Time: 6 minutes

Cooking time: 3 hours

Servings: 6

Smoke Temperature: 180°F and 375°F

Preferred Wood Pellet: Mesquite, Oak

Ingredients:

Lemon slices to garnish

Salt

Pepper

One t. chopped rosemary

3 cloves minced garlic

Zest of one lemon

One t. oregano

Small chopped onion

½ c. white wine

¼ c. olive oil

4 chicken breasts

Directions:

Put the chicken breasts into a large zip-top bag.

In another bowl, put the olive oil, white wine, lemon zest, onion, garlic, oregano, rosemary, pepper, and salt. Stir well to combine.

Coat the chicken in this mixture.

Place into the refrigerator for two to three hours.

Add Preferred Wood Pellet pellets to your smoker and follow your cooker's startup procedure. Preheat your smoker, with your lid closed, until it reaches 350.

The chicken breast should be removed from the bag before patting them dry with paper towels. Place them on the grill and smoke for 15 minutes.

Let it rest for 10 minutes before slicing. Garnish with sliced lemon.

17. Pineapple Turkey Wings

Preparation Time: 15 minutes

Cooking Time: 6 hours

Servings: 6

Smoke Temperature: 180°F and 375°F

Preferred Wood Pellet: Mesquite, Oak

Ingredients:

Pepper

Salt

¼ t. garlic powder

Two pounds turkey wings

One T. packed brown sugar

Two t. chili powder

One 11-ounce cans pineapple, undrained

¼ t. ground ginger

One 11-ounce cans tomato sauce

Directions:

Put the turkey wings into a large dish. Make sure they are in one layer.

In a bowl, put the pepper, salt, garlic powder, ginger, chili powder, brown sugar, pineapple, and tomato sauce. Combine thoroughly.

This mixture should be poured on the turkey.

Place into the refrigerator for four to five hours.

Add Preferred Wood Pellet pellets to your smoker and follow your cooker's startup procedure. Preheat your smoker, with your lid closed, until it reaches 350.

Take the turkey wings out of the marinade. Use the paper towels to pat them dry. Place them onto the grill and smoke for 5 minutes on both sides. Move to cool side and allow smoking for an additional 40 minutes.

Internal Smoke Temperature needs to be 165.

18. Cheesy Turkey Patties

Preparation Time: 10 minutes

Cooking Time: 15 minutes

Servings: 4

Smoke Temperature: 180°F and 375°F

Preferred Wood Pellet: Mesquite, Oak

Ingredients:

Pepper

One t. chili powder

Two wheat pita rounds, cut in half

½ avocado

¼ c. light cream cheese

One tomato

¼ c. shredded cheddar

One cucumber

Two t. chopped green onion

One t. oregano

One-pound ground turkey

Salt

Directions:

Place the oregano, pepper, salt, and turkey into a bowl.

Mix everything with your hands. Form into four patties.

Add Preferred Wood Pellet pellets to your smoker and follow your cooker's startup procedure. Preheat your smoker, with your lid closed, until it reaches 380.

Smoke the patties on the grill. Each side should take approximately five mins.

While patties are cooking, mix the cheddar cheese, cream cheese, chili powder, green onion, and salt.

Slice the pita bread open and spread the mixture onto the inside of the pita. Place a turkey patty inside along with cucumber, tomato, and avocado slices.

19. Chicken Patties

Preparation time: 5 minutes

Cooking Time: 40 minutes

Servings: 6

Smoke Temperature: 180°F and 375°F

Preferred Wood Pellet: Mesquite, Oak

Ingredients:

Pepper

Salt

Two t. paprika

2/3 c. minced onion

Two T. chopped parsley

Two T. lemon juice

One T. chopped cilantro

Pinch red pepper flakes

½ t. cumin

Two T. olive oil

Two pounds ground chicken

Directions:

Wash and finely chop the onions. Mix the onions with the rest of the ingredients

Use your hands and combine all the ingredients. Keep mixing until you have thoroughly mixed all the ingredients. Form into six patties. Refrigerate them for 20 minutes

Add Preferred Wood Pellet pellets to your smoker and follow your cooker's startup procedure. Preheat your smoker, with your lid closed, until it reaches 350.

Smoke each side of the patties on the grill for about ten mins.

Serve on buns with toppings of your choice.

20. Faithfully Italian Herbed Chicken

Preparation Time: 10 minutes

Cooking Time: 4 hours

Servings: 8-10

Smoke Temperature: 180°F and 375°F

Preferred Wood Pellet: Hickory

Ingredients:

1 whole (5 pounds) spatchcocked chicken

2 tablespoons onion powder

2 tablespoons garlic powder

1 tablespoon ground rosemary

1 tablespoon ground parsley

1 lemon, zested

2 teaspoons salt

Directions:

Add Preferred Wood Pellet chips to your smoker and set the Smoke Temperature to 200 degrees F.

Spatchcock the chicken if you have not already.

Take a bowl and mix the dry seasoning and lemon zest.

Rub the blend on both sides of the chicken generously.

Transfer chicken to your smoker (breast side up) and smoke for 4 hours.

Make sure to keep adding more chips every 30-45 minutes.

Once the internal Smoke Temperature of the thickest part registers 165 degrees F, the chicken is ready.

Remove and let it rest for 20 minutes.

Slice and serve.

Enjoy!

21. Maple Smoked Sweet and Spicy Wings

Preparation Time: 30 minutes

Cooking Time: 1½ hours

Servings: 8-10

Smoke Temperature: 180°F and 375°F

Preferred Wood Pellet: Maple

Ingredients:

5 pounds chicken wings

2 and ½ tablespoons black pepper

1 tablespoon onion powder

1 tablespoon garlic salt

1 tablespoon paprika

Sauce

1 cup honey

½ cup spicy BBQ sauce

3 tablespoons apple juice

Directions:

Take a bowl and add pepper, onion powder, garlic salt, and paprika; mix well.

Put wings in a bag and add a spice mix.

Shake and then let sit for 30 minutes.

Add Preferred Wood Pellet chips to your smoker and set the Smoke Temperature to 250 degrees F.

Put meat on the top rack and smoke for 30 minutes.

Turn and smoke for 25 minutes more.

Once the internal Smoke Temperature reaches 160 degrees F, take the meat out.

Take a saucepan and add honey, BBQ sauce, and apple juice over medium-high heat; cook until warm.

Once the wings are ready, transfer them to a foil pan and cover with the sauce.

Return to a smoker (2nd rack) and smoke for 25 minutes more.

Serve and enjoy!

22. Crispy Orange Chicken

Preparation Time: 15 minutes

Cooking Time: 1½-2 hours

Servings: 4

Smoke Temperature: 180°F and 375°F

Preferred Wood Pellet: Apple

Ingredients:

For Poultry Spice Rub

4 teaspoons paprika

1 tablespoon chili powder

2 teaspoons ground cumin

2 teaspoons dried thyme

2 teaspoons salt

2 teaspoons garlic powder

1 teaspoon black pepper

For Marinade

4 chicken quarters

2 cups frozen orange juice concentrate

½ cup soy sauce

1 tablespoon garlic powder

Directions:

Take a small bowl and add all poultry spice rub ingredients listed above; mix well.

Transfer the chicken quarters to a large dish.

Take a medium bowl and whisk in all the marinade ingredients listed above plus half of the spice rub mix.

Spoon the marinade over the chicken and cover.

Refrigerate for 8 hours.

Preheat your smoker to 275 degrees F.

Discard the marinade and rub the surface of the chicken with the remaining spice rub.

Transfer the chicken to smoker and smoke for 1½ to 2 hours.

Remove the chicken from the smoker and check that the internal Smoke Temperature has reached 160 degrees F using a digital thermometer.

Allow it to rest for 10 minutes.

Enjoy!

23. Lovely Smoked Turkey

Preparation Time: 10 minutes

Cooking Time: 4 hours

Servings: 10-12

Smoke Temperature: 180°F and 375°F

Preferred Wood Pellet: Apple

Ingredients:

8 pounds whole turkey, thawed

2 tablespoons extra virgin olive oil

2 tablespoons paprika

2 tablespoons Italian seasoning

1 tablespoon salt

Directions:

Remove the giblets and drain excess juice from the turkey; pat it dry.

Set your smoker to 240 degrees F and add Preferred Wood Pellet chips.

Brush the turkey skin well with olive oil.

Take a bowl and add paprika, Italian seasoning, and salt.

Rub the mixture all over the turkey body.

Add turkey to your smoker and smoke for 4 hours until the internal Smoke Temperature of the thickest part reaches 165 degrees F.

Let it rest for 20 minutes. Slice and serve.

24. Beautiful 5 Spice Duck Breast

Preparation Time: 10 minutes

Cooking Time: 2-3 hours

Servings: 4

Smoke Temperature: 180°F and 375°F

Preferred Wood Pellet: Cherry

Ingredients:

4 (7-ounce each) boneless duck breasts

2 tablespoons salt

2 tablespoons honey

1½ tablespoons five-spice powder

1 tablespoon black pepper

2 tablespoons extra virgin olive oil

Directions:

Trim the duck tendons and make a few slashes into the duck breast skin.

Take a bowl and mix the rub ingredients (except oil), and then rub the duck breasts generously with the mixture.

Drizzle olive oil on both sides of the breasts.

Set your smoker to 250 degrees F and add Preferred Wood Pellet chips.

Add duck and smoke for 2-3 hours until the internal Smoke Temperature reaches your desired state (150 degrees F for medium-well; 165 degrees F for well).

Let it cool and slice.

Enjoy!

Fish and Seafood

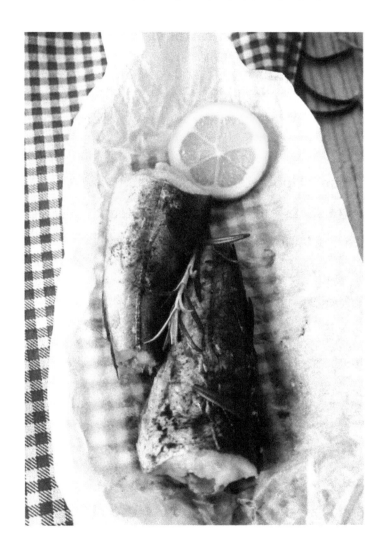

25. Lemon Butter Lobster Tails

Preparation Time: 30 minutes

Cooking Time: 45 minutes -1 hour

Servings: 4

Smoke Temperature: 225°F

Preferred Wood Pellet: Oak or Alder

Ingredients:

4 (8-ounce) lobster tails, fresh (not frozen)

1 cup (2 sticks) unsalted butter, melted, divided

Juice of 2 lemons

1 teaspoon minced garlic

1 teaspoon dried thyme

1 teaspoon dried rosemary

1 teaspoon salt

1 teaspoon freshly ground black pepper

Olive oil, for oiling the grate

¼ cup chopped fresh parsley

Directions:

Following the manufacturer's specific start-up procedure, preheat the smoker to 225°F, and add oak or alder Preferred Wood Pellet.

Split the top of each tail: Grasp the shell and lift it. Using sharp kitchen shears, cut down the middle of the shell, front to back, to the last tail segment. Gently lift the front end of the meat from the shell and rest it on the split shell, leaving the base of the tail attached. Open and rinse out any real grit before smoking.

Cut a slit down the center of the meat to open it up slightly.

In a small bowl, whisk together the butter, lemon juice, garlic, thyme, rosemary, salt, and pepper. Baste each lobster tail with 1 tablespoon of lemon butter.

Oil the grill grate or a nonstick grill mat or perforated pizza screen. Place the tails on the smoker rack split-side up.

Smoke the tails for 45 minutes to 1 hour, basting each with 1 tablespoon of lemon butter once during cooking.

Remove the lobster tails from Preferred Wood Pellet when opaque and firm and the internal Smoke Temperature registers 130°F to 140°F.

Sprinkle the lobster tails with the parsley and serve with the remaining lemon butter for dipping.

26. Smoked Fresh Salmon fillets

Preparation Time: 5 minutes

Cooking Time: 40 Minutes

Servings: 3

Smoke Temperature: 180°F and 375°F

Preferred Wood Pellet: Maple

Ingredients:

1 Salmon fillets (fresh, wild, skin on)

1/3 Teaspoon of Old Bay Seasoning

1 Teaspoon of Basic Seafood Seasoning

Directions:

Pepping for the Grill

Wash salmon fillets fish with cold water and use a paper towel to pat dry

Rub the seasoning on the salmon fillets lightly

Pepping on the Preferred Wood Pellet smoker

Set the Preferred Wood Pellet smoker grill to indirect cooking and preheat to 400°F

Place the fillets skin down directly on the grill grates

Smoke the salmon fillets in the smoker until the internal Smoke Temperature rises to 140°F and fork can easily flake the flesh

Allow the salmon resting for 5 minutes. Serve and enjoy

27. Caribbean Smoked Rockfish

Preparation Time: 10 minutes

Cooking Time: 50 Minutes

Servings: 2

Smoke Temperature: 180°F and 375°F

Preferred Wood Pellet: Maple

Ingredients:

4 Ounces of Pacific Rockfish fillets (fresh, wild)

1 Tablespoon of Caribbean seafood seasoning

2 Teaspoons of extra virgin olive oil (garlic flavored)

Directions:

Pepping for the Grill

Rub olive oil to all sides of the rockfish fillets

Rub the seasoning on the salmon fillets lightly

Pepping on the Pellet Smoker

Set the Smoker grill to indirect cooking and preheat to 225°F

Place the fillets skin down directly on the grill grates

Smoke the salmon fillets in the smoker until the internal Smoke Temperature rises to 140°F and fork can easily flake the flesh

Allow the salmon resting for 5 minutes

Serve and enjoy

28. Smoked Shrimp Tilapia

Preparation time: 5 minutes

Cooking Time: 45 Minutes

Servings: 4

Smoke Temperature: 180°F and 375°F

Preferred Wood Pellet: Maple

Ingredients:

3 Ounces Tilapia fillets (fresh, farmed)

3/4 Teaspoon of Paprika (smoked)

1 Tablespoon of extra virgin olive

3/4 Teaspoon of Basic Seafood Seasoning (Click here)

Ingredients for Shrimp Stuffing:

1/2 Pound of Tail-off Shrimp (cooked, peeled, deveined)

1/2 Cup of Breadcrumbs

1/2 Tablespoon of salted Butter

3/4 Teaspoon of Salt

3/4 Teaspoon of pepper

1 Egg (small, beaten)

1/4 Cup of mayonnaise

3/4 Teaspoon of Parsley (dried)

Directions:

Pepping for the Grill

Pour shrimps into a food processor to chop it finely

Heat olive over medium-high heat in a large skillet, adds butter and melts it, and adds onion and sauté until soft

Place the mixture aside cooling

Combine sautéed mixture, shrimp and the remaining ingredients in a bowl that has cover

Cover it and transfer to the fridge until they are to be used

Rub olive oil on all sides of the fillets

Use a spoon to stuff some great stuffing on the back of each fillet

Spread the stuffing on the back of the fillets

Fold the tilapia fillets into twos and use toothpicks to hold them tight

Spray each of the tilapia with paprika and Basic Seafood Seasoning

Pepping on the Pellet Smoker

Set the Smoker grill to indirect cooking and preheat to 400°F

Transfer the fillet to the nonstick grill tray

Roast the fillets until the internal Smoke Temperature rises to 145°F or for 40 minutes

Allow tilapia fillets resting for 5 minutes

Serve and enjoy

29. Smoked Brined Tuna

Preparation Time: 35 minutes

Cooking Time: 5 Hours

Servings: 2

Smoke Temperature: 180°F and 375°F

Preferred Wood Pellet: Maple

Ingredients:

3 Pounds of Salmon fillets (farmed)

2 Cups of Fresh fish Brine

Directions:

Pepping for the Grill

Cut the fillets into 4 inches sizes so to be able to cook at an equal rate

Put the pork chops into a sealable plastic container and pour into the container Fresh fish Brine

Cover it and place in the fridge overnight

After this duration remove the pork chops and pat dry with paper towels

Use air to dry the salmon fillets

Pepping on the Pellet Smoker

Set the Smoker grill to indirect cooking

Transfer the salmon fillets into Teflon-coated fiberglass mat

Preheat the smoker to 180°F and cook until the internal Smoke Temperature of the salmon fillets rises to 145°F

Remove them from the grill and allow resting for 10 minutes

Serve and enjoy

30. Smoked Sauced Tuna

Preparation Time: 1 hour

Cooking Time: 4 Hours

Servings: 2

Smoke Temperature: 180°F and 375°F

Preferred Wood Pellet: Maple

Ingredients:

10 Ounces Tuna Steaks (fresh)

1 Cup of Teriyaki sauce

Directions:

Pepping for the Grill

Cut the tuna into 4 inches sizes so to be able to cook at an equal rate

Put the tuna steaks into a sealable plastic container and pour into the container Teriyaki sauce

Cover it and place in the fridge for 3 hours

After this duration remove the tuna steaks and pat dry with paper towels

Use air to dry the tuna steaks and put in the refrigerator for another 2 hours

Pepping on the Pellet Smoker

Set the Pellet smoker grill to indirect cooking and preheat to 180°F

Transfer the fillet to nonstick grill tray and place in the smoker for 1 hour

After this time increase Preferred Wood Pellet to 250°F and cook until the internal Smoke Temperature of the tuna rises to 145°F

Remove them from the grill and allow resting for 10 minutes

Serve and enjoy

31. Smoked Brined Trout

Preparation Time: 20 minutes

Cooking Time: 3 Hours

Servings: 3

Smoke Temperature: 180°F and 375°F

Preferred Wood Pellet: Maple

Ingredients:

2 Whole Trout (fresh, skin on, pin bones removed)

3 Cups of Fresh fish Brine

Directions:

Pepping for the Grill

Put the trout into a sealable plastic container and pour into the container Fresh fish Brine

Cover it and place in the fridge for 1 hour

After this duration remove the whole trout and pat dry with paper towels

Use air to dry the salmon fillets and uncover in the fridge and allow for another 1 hour

Pepping on the Pellet Smoker

Set the Pellet smoker grill to indirect cooking and preheat to 180°F

Transfer the fillet to nonstick grill tray and place in the smoker for 1 minute

After this duration transfer the trout to the smoker and increase Preferred Wood Pellet to 225°F

Continue smoking until the internal he of the tuna rises to 145°F

Remove them from the smoker and allow resting for 5 minutes

Serve and enjoy

Vegetables

32. Smoked Vegetable "Potpourri" (Pellet)

Preparation Time: 1 hour

Cooking Time: 1 hour

Servings: 6

Smoke Temperature: 180°F and 375°F

Preferred Wood Pellet: Maple

Ingredients:

2 large zucchinis sliced

2 red bell peppers sliced

2 Russet potatoes sliced

1 red onion sliced

1/2 cup of olive oil

Salt and ground black pepper to taste

Directions:

Start the pellet grill on SMOKE with the lid open until the fire is established. Set the Smoke Temperature to 350 °F and preheat, lid closed, for 10 to 15 minutes.

In the meantime, rinse and slice all vegetables, pat dry on a kitchen paper.

Generously season with the salt and pepper, and drizzle with olive oil.

Place your sliced vegetables into grill basket or onto grill rack and smoke for 40 to 45 minutes. Serve hot.

33. Baked Green Bean Casserole

Preparation Time: 10 minutes

Cooking Time: 50 minutes

Servings: 10-12

Smoke Temperature: 180°F and 375°F

Preferred Wood Pellet: Pecan

Ingredients:

3 lbs. Trimmed Green Beans

Kosher Salt

2 tbsp Olive Oil

2 tbsp Unsalted Butter

1/2 lb. Shitake Mushroom

1/4 cup Shallot

1/4 cup Rice Flour

2 cups Chicken Stock

Directions:

When ready to cook, set the Smoke Temperature to High and preheat, lid closed for 15 minutes.

Fill a large stockpot 2/3 full of water and bring to a boil over high heat. Prepare a large ice bath. When the water is boiling, add 1 Tbsp of salt.

After the water has returned to a rolling boil, add half of the green beans. Cook until al dente, about 2 minutes. Remove with a strainer and place the beans in the ice bath to cool.

Remove the green beans from the water and place on paper towels to dry. Repeat with the remaining green beans. Alternatively, place the green beans on a clean dishcloth and roll up to remove the water.

To make the Sauce: Melt the butter and olive oil in a small saucepan over medium heat. Add the shallots and mushrooms and a generous pinch of salt and cook, stirring, until the mushrooms are soft, about 5 minutes.

Sprinkle the rice flour over the top and stir to coat the mushrooms and cook off the raw flour taste, about 2 minutes. Add the sherry, stir, and reduce, then slowly stir in the stock, allowing to thicken and ensuring there are no lumps, about 3 minutes.

Stir in the cream and Parmigiano-Reggiano. Taste, adding salt and pepper as needed.

Combine the green beans with the sauce. Pour into a large oven-proof serving dish. Sprinkle with almonds. Bake on the Traeger until the sauce is bubbling and the almonds are browned about 30 minutes.

While the green beans are on the grill, fry the shallots. Place the oil in a deep saucepan or Dutch oven and heat oil to 350°F.

Combine the rice flour and salt in a shallow bowl and mix with a fork. Slice the shallots into 1/8-inch rings. Toss the shallots to coat in the rice flour, shaking off any excess in a sieve.

Fry the shallots in batches until golden brown, about 30 seconds to one minute. Drain on paper towels.

When the casserole is ready, garnish with the fried shallots. Enjoy!

34. Mashed Potatoes

Preparation Time: 5 minutes

Cooking Time: 40 minutes

Servings: 8-12

Smoke Temperature: 180°F and 375°F

Preferred Wood Pellet: Hard Wood Pellet or Hickory

Ingredients:

5 lbs. Potatoes

1 1/2 sticks Butter

1 1/2 cup Cream

Kosher Salt

White Pepper

Directions:

When ready to cook, set Smoke Temperature to 300°F and preheat, lid closed for 15 minutes

Peel and dice potatoes into 1/2" cubes.

Place the potatoes in a foil tin and cover. Roast in the Traeger until tender (about 40 minutes).

In a medium saucepan, combine cream and butter. Cook over medium heat until butter is melted.

Mash potatoes using a potato masher. Gradually add in cream and butter mixture, and mix using the masher. Be careful not to overwork, or the potatoes will become gluey. Season with salt and pepper to taste. Enjoy!

35. Corn and Cheese Rellenos

Preparation Time: 30 minutes

Cooking Time: 65 minutes

Servings: 8-12

Smoke Temperature: 180°F and 375°F

Preferred Wood Pellet: Maple and Hard Wood Pellet

Ingredients:

2 lbs. ripe tomatoes

4 cloves garlic

1/2 cup sweet onion

1 jalapeno

1/2 tsp. dry oregano

1 tsp. ground cumin

1 tsp. chile powder

Directions:

Put the tomatoes, garlic, onion, and jalapeno in a shallow baking dish and place on the grill grate before starting your Traeger. (This will expose the vegetables to more Preferred Wood Pellet smoke.)

When ready to cook, start the Traeger grill on Smoke with the lid open until the fire is established (4 to 5 minutes). Set the Smoke Temperature to 450F and preheat, lid closed, for 10 to 15 minutes.

When the grill is hot, arrange the New Mexican chiles and the sweet corn on the grate and grill until the chiles are blistered and blackened in spots and the corn is lightly browned, 15 to 20 minutes for the chiles and 10 to 15 minutes for the corn, turning with tongs as needed.

Stir the tomato-onion mixture once or twice and remove it from the grill grate when the tomatoes begin to break down. Let all the vegetables fresh.

Reduce Preferred Wood Pellet of the Traeger to 350F if you intend to bake the rellenos right away. (You can also make the sauce and assemble the rellenos the day before you bake them. Cover and refrigerate.)

Put the cooled tomato mixture in a blender and liquefy. Pour into a saucepan.

Stir in the cumin, oregano, chile powder, cinnamon, and salt and pepper to taste. Simmer over medium heat for 15 to 20 minutes, or until the sauce is slightly thickened, stirring occasionally.

Carefully peel the blistered outer skin off the New Mexican chiles: Leave the stem ends intact and try not to tear the flesh.

With a small paring knife, slit each chile lengthwise from the shoulder (just below the stem) to the tip. Pull out the seeds and set the chiles aside while you make the filling.

Slice the corn off the cobs and put in a large mixing bowl. Toss with 2 cups of the cheese, reserving 1 cup. Gently stir in the sour cream. Season with salt and pepper. Generously stuff the chiles with the corn-cheese mixture and arrange shoulder to shoulder, cut sides up, in a baking dish or on a rimmed baking sheet. (Line with foil for easy clean-up, if desired.) Sprinkle some of the reserved cheese on top of each relleno.

Bake the rellenos for 25 to 30 minutes, or until the filling is bubbling and the cheese has melted. Reheat the tomato sauce if necessary.

To serve, put a small pool of tomato sauce on each plate and arrange a relleno in the center of it. Sprinkle with queso fresco and garnish with fresh cilantro leaves, if desired. Enjoy!

36. Roasted Tomatoes with Hot Pepper Sauce

Preparation Time: 20 minutes

Cooking Time: 90 minutes

Servings: 4-6

Smoke Temperature: 180°F and 375°F

Preferred Wood Pellet: Hard Wood and Alder

Ingredients:

2 lbs. Tomatoes

3 tbsp. parsley

2 tbsp garlic

Black Pepper

1/2 cup olive oil

Directions:

When ready to cook, set the Smoke Temperature to 400°F and preheat, lid closed for 15 minutes

Wash tomatoes and cut them in half, length width. Place them in a baking dish cut side up.

Sprinkle with chopped parsley, garlic, add salt and black pepper and pour 1/4 cup of olive oil over them.

Place on pre-heated Traeger and bake for 1 1/2 hours. Tomatoes will shrink and the skins will be partly blackened.

Remove tomatoes from baking dish and place in a food processor leaving the cooked oil and puree them.

Drop pasta into boiling salted water and cook until tender. Drain and toss immediately with the pureed tomatoes.

Add the remaining 1/4 cup of raw olive oil and crumbled hot red pepper to taste. Toss and serve. Enjoy!

37. Grilled Fingerling Potato Salad

Preparation Time: 15 minutes

Cooking Time: 15 minutes

Servings: 6-8

Smoke Temperature: 180°F and 375°F

Preferred Wood Pellet: Hard Wood and Pecan

Ingredients:

1-1/2 lbs. potatoes

10 scallions

2 tbsp. rice vinegar

2 tsp. lemon juice

1 jalapeno

2 tsp. Kosher salt

Directions:

When ready to cook, set Smoke Temperature to High and preheat, lid closed for 15 minutes.

Brush the scallions with the oil and place on the grill. Cook until lightly charred, about 2-3 minutes. Remove and let cool. Once the scallions have cooled, slice and set aside.

Brush the Fingerlings with oil (reserving 1/3 cup for later use), then salt and pepper. Place cut side down on the grill until cooked through, about 4-5 minutes.

In a bowl, whisk the remaining 1/3 cup olive oil, rice vinegar, salt, and lemon juice, then mix in the scallions, potatoes, and sliced jalapeno.

Season with salt and pepper and serve. Enjoy!

38. Smoked Jalapeno Poppers

Preparation Time: 15 minutes

Cooking Time: 60 minutes

Servings: 4-6

Smoke Temperature: 180°F and 375°F

Preferred Wood Pellet: Hard Wood and Mesquite

Ingredients:

12 jalapenos

6 slices bacon

8 oz cream cheese

Direction

When ready to cook, set Smoke Temperature to 180°F and preheat, lid closed for 15 minutes.

Slice the jalapeños in half lengthwise. Scrape out any seeds and ribs with a small spoon or paring knife.

Mix softened cream cheese with Traeger Pork & Poultry rub and grated cheese.

Spoon mixture onto each jalapeño half. Wrap with bacon and secure with a toothpick.

Place the jalapeños on a rimmed baking sheet. Place on grill and smoke for 30 minutes.

Increase the grill Smoke Temperature to 375°F and cook an additional 30 minutes or until bacon is cooked to desired doneness. Serve warm, enjoy!

Other Meats

39. Grilled Wild Goose Breast in Beer Marinade

Preparation Time: 2 hours

Cooking Time: 50 minutes

Servings: 4

Smoke Temperature: 180°F and 375°F

Preferred Wood Pellet: Maple

Ingredients:

4 goose breasts

2 cups beer of your choice

1 1/2 tsp Worcestershire sauce

1 tsp garlic powder

1/2 tsp paprika

Salt and pepper

Directions:

Place the goose breasts in a Ziploc plastic bag.

Pour in the beer, Worcestershire sauce, garlic powder, paprika, and salt and pepper. Close the bag and shake to combine all ingredients well.

Marinate in refrigerated for 2 hours.

Remove the goose meat from marinade and pat dry on kitchen towel (reserve the marinade).

Preheat a grill for medium heat, about 300 degrees F.

Place the goose breasts on the grate. Brush occasionally with the marinade only for the first half an hour.

Continue to cook for 10 - 15 minutes longer or until reach an internal Smoke Temperature of 165 degrees F.

Serve hot.

40. Grilled Wild Rabbit with Rosemary and Garlic

Preparation Time: 15 minutes

Cooking Time: 1 hour

Servings: 4

Smoke Temperature: 180°F and 375°F

Preferred Wood Pellet: Maple

Ingredients:

1 - 2 wild rabbits (about 2 pounds)

2 cloves of garlic, melted

2 tbsp of rosemary dried, crushed

Juice from 1 lemon

1/4 cup olive oil

Salt and freshly ground pepper

Directions:

If we use a whole rabbit, cut into portions as follows: cut up a rabbit by removing the front legs, which are not attached to the body by bone.

Slide your knife up from underneath, along the ribs, and slice through. Cut the trunk into slices of 4-5 cm thick.

In a bowl, mix the garlic, rosemary, oil, salt and pepper, and lemon juice.

Brush the rabbit pieces with the garlic-rosemary mixtures.

Start the pellet grill to pre-heat to 300 degrees and preheat, lid closed, for 10 to 15 minutes.

Lay the rabbit pieces onto grill rack.

Grill for about 12 - 15 minutes per side, or until the meat is no longer pink inside.

Serve.

41. Smoked Aromatic Pheasant on Pellet Grill

Preparation time: 30 minutes

Cooking Time: 5 hours

Servings: 4

Smoke Temperature: 180°F and 375°F

Preferred Wood Pellet: Maple

Ingredients:

1 large pheasant

3/4 cup fresh butter

1 tsp fresh basil, finely chopped

1 tsp fresh thyme, finely chopped

1 tsp parsley, finely chopped

Salt and ground pepper

1/2 cup white wine

Directions:

Wash the pheasant, pat dry with a paper towel, and tie cross its legs.

In a small saucepan melt the butter over medium heat.

Add the basil, parsley and thyme, wine and salt and pepper; stir well and remove from heat.

Brush the pheasant generously with the herbed butter mixtures.

Start your pellet grill, and set the Smoke Temperature to 350F and preheat, lid closed, for 10 to 15 minutes.

Smoke the pheasant 3 hours - 5 hours.

When the pheasant reaches an internal Smoke Temperature of 160°F in the thigh meat, take out of the smoker.

Chop the pheasant and serve hot.

42. Stuffed Wild Duck on Pellet Grill

Preparation Time: 2 hours

Cooking Time: 2 hours

Servings: 6

Smoke Temperature: 180°F and 375°F

Preferred Wood Pellet: Maple

Ingredients:

1 wild duck (about 4 pounds), cleaned

1 mushroom cut into slices

1 tsp fresh parsley, finely chopped

1/2 tsp of thyme

1/4 cup fresh butter

Salt and pepper

Directions:

In a bowl, combine mushrooms, parsley, thyme, fresh butter and salt and pepper.

Place the mushrooms mixture in the wild duck belly.

Start the pellet grill on Smoke with the lid open until the fire is established (4 to 5 minutes).

Set the Smoke Temperature to 350F and preheat, lid closed, for 10 to 15 minutes.

Place the duck directly on the grill grate.

Cover the grill and cook the duck for 1-1/2 hours.

After 1-1/2 hours, drain the juices and fat from the pan and flip the duck, breast side down.

Let the duck cool down, pull the twigs, and serve.

Rubs and Sauces

43. Ginger Dipping Sauce

Preparation Time: 10 Minutes

Cooking Time: 30 Minutes

Servings: 4

Ingredients:

6 tablespoons ponzu sauce

2 tablespoons scallions

2 tsp ginger

2 tsp mirin

1 tsp sesame oil

¼ tsp salt

Directions:

In a blender place all ingredients and blend until smooth

Pour smoothie in a glass and serve

44. Thai Dipping Sauce

Preparation Time: 10 Minutes

Cooking Time: 30 Minutes

Servings: 4

Ingredients:

6 tsp garlic sauce

2 tablespoons fish sauce

2 tablespoons lime juice

1 tablespoon brown sugar

1 tsp chili flakes

Directions:

In a blender place all ingredients and blend until smooth

Pour smoothie in a glass and serve

45. Coconut Dipping Sauce

Preparation Time: 10 Minutes

Cooking Time: 30 Minutes

Servings: 4

Ingredients:

4 tablespoons coconut milk

1 tablespoon curry paste

2 tablespoons lime juice

2 tsp soy sauce

1 tsp fish sauce

1 tsp honey

Directions:

In a blender place all ingredients and blend until smooth

Pour smoothie in a glass and serve

46. Black Bean Dipping Sauce

Preparation Time: 10 Minutes

Cooking Time: 30 Minutes

Servings: 4

Ingredients:

2 tablespoons black bean paste

2 tablespoons peanut butter

1 tablespoon maple syrup

2 tablespoons olive oil

Directions:

In a blender place all ingredients and blend until smooth

Pour smoothie in a glass and serve

47. Maple Syrup Dipping Sauce

Preparation Time: 10 Minutes

Cooking Time: 30 Minutes

Servings: 4

Ingredients:

2 tablespoons peanut butter

2 tablespoons maple syrup

2 tsp olive oil

2 tablespoon Korean black bean paste

Directions:

In a blender place all ingredients and blend until smooth

Pour smoothie in a glass and serve

48. Soy Dipping Sauce

Preparation Time: 10 Minutes

Cooking Time: 30 Minutes

Servings: 4

Ingredients:

¼ cup soy sauce

¼ cup sugar

¼ cup rice vinegar

½ cup scallions

½ cup cilantro

Directions:

In a blender place all ingredients and blend until smooth

Pour smoothie in a glass and serve

49. Avocado Salsa

Preparation Time: 10 Minutes

Cooking Time: 30 Minutes

Servings: 4

Ingredients:

2 avocados

1 onion

1 jalapeno

2 garlic cloves

¼ cup red wine vinegar

1 tablespoon lime juice

¼ cup parsley leaves

Directions:

In a blender place all ingredients and blend until smooth

Pour smoothie in a glass and serve

50. Barbeque Sauce

Preparation Time: 10 Minutes

Cooking Time: 30 Minutes

Servings: 4

Ingredients:

¼ cup ketchup

1 tablespoon brown sugar

1 tsp molasses

1 tsp hot sauce

1 tsp mustard

1 tsp onion powder

Directions:

In a blender place all ingredients and blend until smooth

Pour smoothie in a glass and serve